how diablo became Spirit

to all who listen

© July 2020 Conscious Stories LLC
Book 11

Illustrations by Alexis Aronson

Published by
Conscious Stories
350 E. Royal Lane
Suite #150
Irving, TX 75039

Legally speaking all rights are reserved, so this book may not be reproduced without the express written consent of the publisher. On a relational level, this book can be read to inspire, engage and connect parents and children. That is what it was made for, so please read the story and be kind enough to give a mention to Andrew Newman and Conscious Stories.

www.consciousstories.com

First Edition

ISBN 978-1-943750-16-0

Library of Congress
Control Number:
2017902250

The last 20 minutes of every day are precious.

Dear parents, teachers, and readers,

This story has been gift-wrapped with two simple mindfulness practices to help you connect more deeply with your children in the last 20 minutes of each day.

● Quietly set your intention for calm and open, connection.

● Then start your story time with the **Snuggle Breathing Meditation**. Read each line aloud and take slow, deep breaths together in order to relax and be present.

● At the end of the story, you will find **Spirit's Secret Steps**. These steps will help you to communicate with animals. Remember the more you practice, the easier it becomes.

Enjoy snuggling into togetherness!

Andrew

An easy breathing meditation
Snuggle Breathing

Our story begins with us breathing together.
Say each line aloud and then
take a slow deep breath in and out.

I breathe for me

I breathe for you

I breathe for us

I breathe for all that surrounds us

Hi, my name is Spirit.

I'm a big black leopard, and I live at the Jukani Wildlife Sanctuary in South Africa.

I wasn't always known as Spirit, and I haven't always been this friendly and chatty.

My first home was in a cage.
I was sad and lonely there.

People demanded a lot of me,
and I never felt loved or seen
for who I really am.

I was called Diablo because I was big
and fierce.

You may not know this, but the word
Diablo is Spanish; it means 'the devil.'

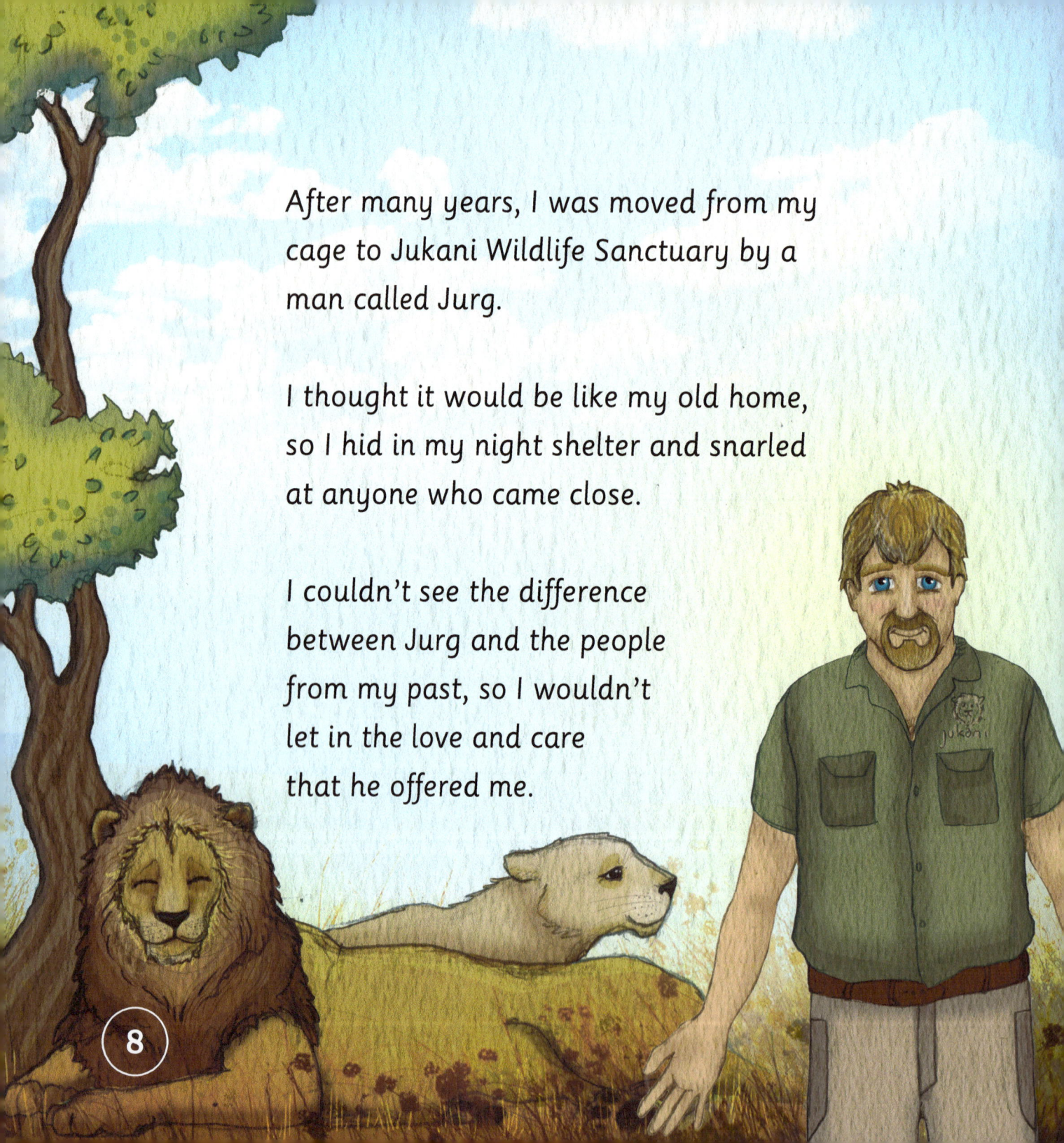

After many years, I was moved from my cage to Jukani Wildlife Sanctuary by a man called Jurg.

I thought it would be like my old home, so I hid in my night shelter and snarled at anyone who came close.

I couldn't see the difference between Jurg and the people from my past, so I wouldn't let in the love and care that he offered me.

He also called me Diablo.
But I never felt like the devil inside.

I was surprised one day when a woman called Anna came to my hiding place.

I watched Anna slow her breathing, clear her mind, and open her heart to connect with me.

Anna asked, "How do you feel about being here?"

"Is there anything you want to tell me?"

Most importantly, she asked, "What do you need to be happy?"

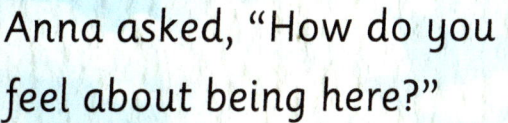

To the outside world it looked like a woman
sitting quietly next to a big black cat.
But magically, the space between us filled
with my answers that Anna could understand.

Sometimes she heard words.
Sometimes images appeared in her mind, and
sometimes feelings showed up in her body.

"They have me all wrong," I said.

"It is my nature to be fierce because I am a leopard.

I am wise and deserving of respect and recognition as the powerful spirit that I am. The name Diablo does not fit my true nature. I want it changed."

I could hardly believe it when Jurg came and spoke directly to me that same day. He had never done that before.

"You're so beautiful," he said.
"Haaw," I grunted.

"I don't expect anything of you. You don't have to come out of your night shelter at all."
"Haaw."

"I won't make any demands of you. We will respect your wishes."
"Haaw."

I'm not sure if it was my heart or his heart that softened first, but things became different between us.

One by one, Jurg spoke about all the problems I had shared with Anna.

I was particularly worried about two special cubs who shared the neighboring cage in my old zoo.

I'd thought of them often and wondered what happened to them.

I was so comforted when Jurg told me, "Those two cubs you asked about are safe."

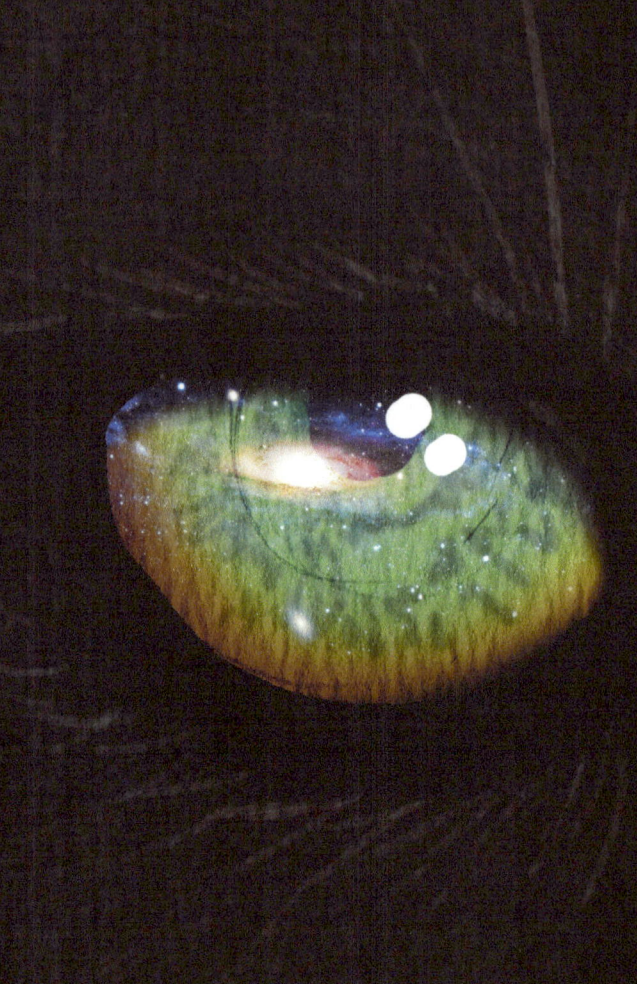

Then Jurg said, "I do not see you as the devil. You are a magnificent black leopard. You are wise and deserve our respect and recognition.

From now on, we will call you **Spirit**."

I loved my new name from the first moment
I heard it. It's exactly who I am.

That day I walked out of my hiding place into a new world of friendship and happiness.

I have been happy ever since.

That's my story.

I hope it encourages animals to trust humans and helps humans to remember that we can all talk to each other.

Much love and special leopard purrs,

"Haaw."

– Spirit

Listening is a gift.

Everybody has the ability to connect with animals. It just takes clear intention, an open heart, and a little practice.

Luckily Spirit and Anna have shared their secret steps for you to practice.

Have fun! A little bit of playfulness will help

Connecting with animals
Spirit's Secret Steps

1
Set your intention

Fill in the blank with your favorite animal. Say quietly inside, "I connect heart to heart with _____."

2
Clear your mind

Sigh deeply three times to begin. Relax your whole body.

6
Ask one question at a time

"Is there anything you want to tell me?"

7
Listen patiently

Listen with your heart, and wait for their answer. Do you hear any words? Do you see any pictures? Do you feel something change in your body?

3

Open your heart

Put your hand on your heart, close your eyes, and breathe into your heartspace until you feel warm and comfortable.

4

Begin connecting

Imagine a golden thread of love connecting from your heart to theirs.

5

Say Hello

Silently say "Hello." If you know their name, use it.

8

Don't assume. Be curious.

Don't assume you know the answers. Be curious and let the animal share their truth – even if it isn't what you expected.

9

Say thank you

When your conversation has ended, say "Thank you" to the animal and to your own heart.

10

Share what you discovered

Tell a friend, or write it down.

About Anna

Anna Breytenbach is a professional animal communicator who has received advanced training from the Assisi International Animal Institute in California, USA. She has been practicing and teaching across the globe for 15 years. She's also the subject of the documentary film, **The Animal Communicator**, which has reached over 10 million viewers online.

Anna's goal is to raise awareness and advance the relationships among human and nonhuman animals, on both the personal and spiritual levels. She guides workshop participants to develop their natural senses and deepen their connection with all species in an honouring manner. In her communication and conservation work, she is inspired by being a voice for the animals and natural environments.

www.animalspirit.org

About Jurg and Karen Olsen

Jurg and Karen Olsen founded Jukani Animal Sanctuary in 2005. Their passion for big cats and determination to make a difference in a heartless industry led them to start Jukani, with three lions and a tiger bought and rescued from a lion breeding farm.

All of the animals they brought to Jukani were in need of a better life. The Sanctuary is home to a variety of big cats (including Spirit) and other wildlife species. Jukani focuses on conservation education, especially the plight of large predators in captivity, in South Africa and all over the world.

www.jukani.co.za

Watch the video

The incredible story of how leopard Diablo became Spirit.

Special Acknowledgements

The Foster brothers and the team at **www.senseafrica.com** for their excellence in filming **"The Animal Communicator"** • NHU-Africa for commissioning the **"The Animal Communicator"** • Jessie Rose for her ongoing support in many ways.

A collection of stories with wise and lovable characters who teach spiritual values to your children

Helping you connect more deeply in the last 20 minutes of the day

 **Stories with purpose**
Lovable characters who overcome life's challenges to find peace, love and connection.

 **Reflective activity pages**
Cherish open sharing time with your children at the end of each day.

 **Simple mindfulness practices**
Enjoy easy breathing practices that soften the atmosphere and create deep connection when reading together.

 **Supportive parenting community**
Join a community of conscious parents who seek connection with their children.

Free downloadable coloring pages
Visit www.consciousstories.com

 #ConsciousBedtimeStories   @ConsciousBedtimeStories

Andrew Newman - author

Andrew Newman is the award-winning author and founder of www.ConsciousStories.com, a growing series of bedtime stories purpose-built to support parent-child connection in the last 20 minutes of the day. His professional background includes deep training in therapeutic healing work and mindfulness. He brings a calm yet playful energy to speaking events and workshops, inviting and encouraging the creativity of his audiences, children K-5, parents, and teachers alike.

Andrew has been an opening speaker for Deepak Chopra, a TEDx presenter in Findhorn, Scotland and author-in-residence at the Bixby School in Boulder, Colorado. He is a graduate of The Barbara Brennan School of Healing, a Non-Dual Kabbalistic healer and has been actively involved in men's work through the Mankind Project since 2006. He counsels parents, helping them to return to their center, so they can be more deeply present with their kids.

 "Why the last 20 minutes of the day matter"

Alexis Aronson — illustrator

Alexis is a self-taught illustrator, designer and artist from Cape Town, South Africa. She has a passion for serving projects with a visionary twist that incorporate image making with the growth of human consciousness for broader impact. Her media range from digital illustration and design to fine art techniques, such as intaglio printmaking, ceramic sculpture, and painting. In between working for clients and creating her own art for exhibition, Alexis is an avid nature lover, swimmer, yogi, hiker, and gardener.

www.alexisaronson.com

Star Counter

Every time you breathe together and read aloud, you make a star shine in the night sky.

Color in a star to count how many times you have read this book.

SCAN AND WIN!
Scan this QR code to win awesome prizes!

www.ingramcontent.com/pod-product-compliance
Lightning Source LLC
Chambersburg PA
CBHW040458240426
43665CB00042B/68